Prolance

www.prolancewriting.com
California, USA
©2017 Mai Hazem
Illustrations ©2017 Ahmed Moneer

ISBN: 978-0-9962457-9-1
Printed in USA

Hannah Travels to Japan

By Mai Hazem

Art by Ahmed Moneer

Prolance

Dedicated to: My family;
thank you for always
pushing me to do every
little thing I dream of.

Today is Hannah's first day of third grade. On her way to school, Hannah could feel a little rumble in her tummy. Her mommy had explained that she had butterflies, which meant she was nervous about her first day.

But mommy reassured her that her new teacher, Miss Jules, was very nice, and that Hannah would make lots of new friends.

When Hannah got to her new class, Miss Jules told all the students to pick a cubie where they could leave their lunch packs and jackets until they needed them.

After Hannah put her stuff away, she quickly found her desk and sat down. As all the students began to take their seats, a little boy came and sat at the desk next to Hannah.

"Hello," the little boy said to Hannah.

"My name is Naoki."

"Hello, I'm Hannah," she replied.

"My family and I just moved here from Japan," Naoki said. "I'm very excited to make new friends here."

"Oh that is exciting!" exclaimed Hannah. "I've never been outside California. Where is Japan?"

"Japan is near Asia." Naoki stated as he pointed up to the large map hanging on the classroom wall.

"It's actually an island. Would you like to go see it? I can show you around!"

"Really?" Hannah asked. "But how would we get there?"

"Easy!" said Naoki. "We'll just jump in!"

Hannah and Naoki stood up from their desks and went to stand in front of the big map. They stood right in front of Japan on the map, closed their eyes, and **JUMPED!**

When Hannah opened her eyes, she wasn't in their classroom anymore, but her new friend Naoki was still there with her.

"We're here!" said Naoki. "This is Japan."

Hannah looked around and could see everything was different from what she was used to.

"Come on," exclaimed Naoki, "I'll show you around!"

Together they went off towards a busy street full of people walking around and riding their bikes back and forth. As they were walking, Naoki said, "Konnichiwa" to someone.

"What does that mean?" asked Hannah.

"Oh, that is how we say 'hello' in Japanese," explained Naoki.

"Konnichiwa," Hannah repeated.

As they walked along, Hannah could smell something wonderful coming from people's homes.

"What is that terrific smell?" She asked Naoki.

"That's breakfast!" he said. "We'll go to my family's house and have some white rice, fried egg, and natto, which is a soybean. It's really good!"

So Hannah followed Noaki until they got to his house.

Once inside, Hannah and Naoki took off their shoes at the entrance. Naoki explained that it was a Japanese custom for everyone to do so.

Hannah greeted Naoki's family by saying, "Konnichiwa," and imitated Naoki as he gave his parents and grandparents a respectful bow.

Then they all sat on the floor around a low table and enjoyed a delicious breakfast of white rice, fried egg, and natto.

After they had finished their meal, Hannah and Naoki said, "Sayonara," meaning goodbye, to Naoki's family, and went out to see more of Japan.

As they walked along, Naoki explained to Hannah that he lived with both his parents and grandparents, and that in Japan it was common and even expected for grandparents to live in the same house with you. Hannah loved the idea of her grandparents living with them.

She told Naoki her grandparents enjoyed living in Florida and she usually saw them during the holidays.

Just then, a woman wearing a very pretty dress walked by them.

"Wow!" exclaimed Hannah, "That is a pretty dress!" She admired the bright red color and beautiful design of the dress as the lady passed.

"That is called a kimono," Naoki replied. "They are usually worn for special events.

Now let's go, I want to show you something cool before we go!"

And with that, Naoki took off running.

Hannah followed quickly and the two continued to run until they found themselves in front of a big wooden building that looked like an oversized house.

"Wow!" exclaimed Hannah as she tilted her head back to look up at the huge place.

"This is called the Todaiji Temple," Naoki said. "It is over a thousand years old!"

All around the temple Hannah could see beautiful gardens, and even found some deer freely roaming around!

Suddenly Hannah could hear a ringing sound. As she looked over to Naoki, the sound grew louder.

"Alright kids let's all settle down now," she could hear Miss Jules voice!

And just like that, with the blink of an eye, Hannah was back at her desk in class, with Naoki at the desk next to her! The two smiled wide at each other.

"That was so much fun!" Hannah exclaimed as Miss Jules began class, and Naoki nodded in agreement.

Hannah looked around at the rest of her classmates and wondered what other surprises third grade had in store for her. She couldn't wait to find out!

About the author:
Mai Hazem is a mother, wife, sister, daughter, and friend with a passion for reading, writing, poetry and art. She has a Bachelors of Mass Communications from California State University, Fullerton.

"The purpose of my stories is to grasp the diversity we see in today's classrooms, as they are filled with kids from all different parts of the world. There is a goal to educate kids about the cultures their classmates come from. It is done in the hope of not only educating and informing young minds, both geographically and culturally, but also opening hearts to acceptance of what may be perceived as 'different.' By starting at a young age, we decrease the borders of the future and bring us closer to being one world, one people."

www.ingramcontent.com/pod-product-compliance
Lightning Source LLC
Chambersburg PA
CBHW081234020426
42331CB00012B/3174